Original title:
Poppy Pathways

Copyright © 2025 Creative Arts Management OÜ
All rights reserved.

Author: Ethan Prescott
ISBN HARDBACK: 978-1-80567-019-3
ISBN PAPERBACK: 978-1-80567-099-5

Crimson Trails of Memory

In a field where laughter grows,
Forgotten socks and garden gnomes.
Chasing vines with silly prances,
We dance like ants in silly romps.

A ladybug steals my snack,
I swat at it, it won't hold back.
We giggle at the bumblebee,
Who buzzes loudly, then takes a tea.

Blossoms Beneath the Sky

Butterflies add flair to the show,
As we tumble through the petals below.
A sunflower winks and teases me,
I stab a toe on its root, oh glee!

Sneaky ants march in a line,
They swipe my sandwich, think it's fine.
We laugh as their parade holds sway,
But I let them win—always play!

Whispers in the Wildflower Wind

The daisies whisper jokes at dusk,
While we jump, avoiding the musk.
A frog joins in with a ribbit cheer,
As we twirl to tunes, loud and clear.

A dandelion sends its wish,
To hop along and dance, oh bliss.
We twine our hands, all skin and grass,
While a breeze teases, as we pass.

The Fields of Remembrance

In fields where laughter grows so bright,
   We roll and tumble, pure delight.
   The clouds above wear silly hats,
   While rabbits giggle at the bats.

Oh, what a show, this charming spree,
   With floppy ears and glee at sea.
   We toast to flowers, toast to bees,
And laugh till we fall—oh, how it frees!

The Color of Hopeful Tomorrows

In a field where colors dance,
Oh look, a bee in its prance!
With petals bright, they wave and cheer,
Say hi to the next flower near!

A squirrel wearing a sun hat,
Checks if the flowers like to chat.
They giggle with a breeze so light,
And turn the day from dull to bright!

Fields of Red and Gold

In crimson gowns and golden crowns,
The flowers play their silly clowns.
A wind gusts through with joy and cheer,
Their laughter rings to every ear!

A rabbit hops with endless glee,
Confused, he thinks he's royalty!
He bows to blooms, takes a short nap,
Dreaming of veggies, what a trap!

Footprints on a Floral Route

Along the path where flowers bloom,
A dog rolls past, he smells the room.
With muddy paws and sunshine bright,
He stops to dance, oh what a sight!

The ladybugs in tiny cars,
Streak by below, like racing stars.
With tiny horns, they honk and speed,
What a wild floral race indeed!

Serenade of the Swaying Stems

The stems sway to a funny song,
As grasshoppers sing loud and strong.
They tap their feet and jiggle too,
Creating joy in skies so blue!

A playful frog jumps left and right,
His tiny leaps are such a sight!
With every hop, he finds a friend,
In silly songs that never end!

The Charms of Flourishing Paths

When flowers laugh and play in bloom,
Their dance brings joy, dispelling gloom.
A bumblebee can't find his way,
He buzzes round, oh what a day!

The squirrels talk of secret seeds,
While chattering about their needs.
With petals bright and colors bold,
They tell of tales that never grow old.

The sun sips tea and cracks a joke,
As shadows stretch and laughter stoke.
Each pathway twists and spirals up,
A carousel in bright green cup.

In leafy hats and flowery shoes,
They prance about with silly views.
With every step, a giggle spreads,
In charming lanes, where fun embeds.

Echoes of Fiery Circumstance

A fiery sun begins to blaze,
While flowers dance in silly ways.
Red petals twirl, a wild ballet,
As rabbits hop and shout hooray!

In the garden's gentle light,
A caterpillar takes to flight.
He stumbles on a clumsy leaf,
And laughs out loud, beyond belief!

The ants parade with pomp and cheer,
Each tiny soldier feeling queer.
They juggle crumbs like circus acts,
While onlookers share goofy hacks.

A gopher in a fancy hat,
Recites tall tales of this and that.
With every chuckle, blooms unfold,
In echoes bright, their fun retold.

Tales Written in the Red Bellows

In tulip towns where giggles dwell,
The flowers weave their funny spell.
Each bud unlocks a cheerful grin,
With stories wild that never thin.

A ladybug plays hide and seek,
Amongst the blooms, oh what a cheek!
She trips on leaves, does a little twirl,
And sends her friends into a whirl.

The daisies rock and twist with glee,
While butterflies sip honey tea.
They gossip fast about the bee,
And chuckle at his clumsiness spree.

With wild Redcoats in a grand parade,
They dance along the leafy glade.
In every tale, a laugh and shout,
Their joyous hearts, what life's about!

The Silent Murmur of Blossoms

In quiet nooks where colors shine,
The blooms conspire, feeling fine.
A whisper here, a chuckle there,
   As petals flutter in the air.

The garden holds a secret game,
Where every flower plays its name.
With each soft rustle, laughter spills,
   As nature hums its funny thrills.

A dandelion with goofy dreams,
Decides to float upon moonbeams.
He makes a wish on winds so bold,
And teases clouds with stories untold.

Beneath the sky, shadows play tricks,
As flowers bend and laugh in clicks.
In every murmur, joy does bloom,
A symphony that breaks the gloom.

Steps on Soft Vermilion Carpet

Each step I take, I can't believe,
It squishes down, makes me retrieve.
A squishy sound beneath my shoe,
Is this a joke or a flavor, too?

With every bounce, I sense the thrill,
Like jelly beans that dance at will.
The ground rejoices, soft and bright,
Beneath my feet, such pure delight.

I skip and hop, my spirit's light,
Like jumping beans in sunny flight.
What's that? A wispy hint of glee?
Careful, or I'll slip, just wait and see!

A vermilion floor, a clown's parade,
With giggles sparkling as I wade.
I trip and land, oh what a mess,
At least the ground's a comfy dress!

The Beckoning of Flora's Embrace

Oh flowers grin with silly faces,
They beckon me with leafy paces,
Join in the dance, the pollen spins,
A game of tickle, where sneezing wins!

The blooms await, their petals wide,
Inviting me for a frolic ride.
A bee's a jester, buzzing cheer,
While butterflies giggle, never fear!

I dip and dive, the petals sway,
Each bloom a friend who loves to play.
The flowers' laughter fills the air,
A ticklish trap beyond compare!

But oops! I fell into a patch,
With petals soft, a floral catch.
I laugh aloud, can't help but find,
Nature's pranks are oh-so-kind!

Lush Labyrinths of Red Elegance

In gardens vast, I roam around,
A maze of crimson, joy unbound.
Lost in bright hues, I seek a way,
With giggles spilling every day.

A twist and turn, oh where's the door?
Each path leads to more laughs galore.
The velvet blooms tease me to wander,
In this red labyrinth, I ponder.

A wanderer's joy, I twirl and spin,
Chasing petals, where do I begin?
The flowers whisper secrets neat,
In giggly tones, they dance my beat.

I bump a wall, giggling still,
Is this a maze or a playful thrill?
Each turn's a joke, a friendly trap,
In red elegance, I'm lost, no map!

Whispers of the Gentle Breeze

A whisper floats, a breeze so sly,
Encourages me to leap and fly.
It tickles grass and tousles hair,
Like giggling sprites playing fair.

Each gust arrives with a playful nudge,
Come dance, dear friend, no need to grudge.
We twirl among the petals bright,
With laughter soaring, such pure delight.

The breeze, a jester, comes and goes,
It rustles leaves, a playful prose.
"Catch me if you can!" it seems to tease,
While I try hard to swerve with ease.

A sum of giggles in the air,
Tangled laughter everywhere.
Oh gentle breeze, let's laugh away,
In fragile whispers, let's play today!

A Scenic Route of Embered Dreams

In a land where giggles grow,
Each step's a joke, a delight to show.
Pathways glow in a fiery hue,
Tickling our feet, like a ticklish shoe.

We dance on clouds of crimson cheer,
Every turn brings laughter near.
With painted skies, we sing a tune,
A serenade to a silly moon.

The trees wear hats, a funny sight,
Wave to the branches, with pure delight.
Bouncing berries chase the sun,
Chasing each other, just for fun.

Misplaced squirrels toss acorns wide,
While breezes join the silly ride.
In embered dreams, the world's a jest,
Where laughter blooms and takes a rest.

The Road of Passionate Blooms

Strolling where the colors burst,
With petals dancing, oh how they thirst!
Each flower winks with cheeky grace,
As bees perform a jitterbug race.

Butterflies wear their finest threads,
Chasing sunbeams, avoiding beds.
Every blossom has a tale to spin,
With giggles woven deep within.

The roots are tangled in a jig,
While ants hold tiny coffee gigs.
A crocus yells, 'I'm the star!',
With daffodils cheering from afar.

On this merry path of hues,
We share our jokes, we share our views.
As blooms embrace the winding ways,
We laugh till dusk, in joyous plays.

Fluttering Wings Over Scarlet Ground

In a flurry of red, the laughter flies,
With wings that tickle the bluest skies.
Each flap and flutter tells us where,
The breeze brings chuckles, light as air.

Chasing shadows, the critters grin,
As giggles echo from within.
A lively throng of colors bright,
Spreading joy and comedic light.

The ground is soft with a squishy charm,
As fairies dance without alarm.
Hopscotch on petals, a quirky feat,
Landing on laughter and dance of feet.

While wings are whirling, the world ignites,
In a raucous whirl of floral delights.
As laughter twirls above the ground,
In joyous chaos, bliss resounds.

The Allure of Blushing Trails

A pathway paved with rosy schemes,
Where humor blossoms in funny themes.
Each step a giggle, each turn a laugh,
As flowers plot their silly math.

Backwards bumbles of bees parade,
In pollen contests, they've all played.
The petals blush as pranks unfold,
With tales of mischief, brave and bold.

Over hills of silly hues,
Where daisies tell their humorous news.
Rainbow rabbits hop and tease,
In a whimsical dance to please.

With every twist, a joke awaits,
The whispering wind celebrates.
In blushing trails of jest and cheer,
We stroll with laughter, year after year.

A Canvas of Red Horizons

In fields of red, I trip and tumble,
Chasing dreams and avoiding the fumble.
Colors dance beneath the sun,
Who knew a flower could weigh a ton?

A ladybug flies, I start to giggle,
Why does it move like it's ready to wiggle?
With petals swirling 'round my head,
I've never seen red look so well-fed!

Grass stains on jeans, oh what a sight,
I'm the clown in this floral fight.
But just as I pose for a selfie,
A bee zooms by—what a smelly help-y!

So here I am, in a field of glee,
With flowers laughing and rolling in spree.
Together we create a silly ballet,
In this wild garden, I'm never cliché!

Glimpses of Petal-Laden Trails

On trails where blossoms sprout and sway,
I skipped along, come what may.
But wait, what's that? A flower sneezed!
A pollen storm that left me wheezed!

I saw a squirrel with a flower crown,
Does he think he's the king of the town?
With nuts and petals, in his grasp,
I laughed so hard, I nearly gasped!

A butterfly winks, it's quite the flirt,
While I'm here in dirt, oh what a dirt!
Chasing whimsy in a petal trail,
Like a giddy sailor, I set my sail.

With giggles trailing in the morning breeze,
I tumble through blooms, oh such sweet tease!
Each flower whispers secrets untold,
Life's a jest, and I'm feeling bold!

Footsteps on the Scarlet Journey

Steps in red where blooms abound,
With laughter echoing all around.
Each petal whispers, 'What a treat!'
Watch your step or you might meet!

A bumblebee buzzes, wearing a frown,
"Why is this human messing my crown?"
But I just giggle, it's all in fun,
He's the ruler of this floral run!

I stumbled once, then twice, then thrice,
These flowers really do look nice.
With each misstep, I twirl and laugh,
Taking on a nature-made photograph.

Folks take pictures, but I'm the show,
Juggling daisies—now that's a pro!
On this silly journey, I'm dancing free,
In this garden, it's just flowers and me!

Beneath the Sunlit Canopy

Under skies where daisies cheer,
I ventured forth to spread some cheer.
But oh dear me, what's that I see?
A squirrel stealing my picnic brie!

With grapes and crumbs, all in a heap,
The sneaky little guy takes his leap.
I shake my head, he's quite the thief,
But his antics bring me such relief!

While butterflies dance in a sunlit spree,
I'm left to ponder my stolen brie.
With wagging tails and plucky feet,
I join the flowers in a goofy feat.

A merry band of blossoms bright,
Under the sun, it's quite the sight.
Life's got its quirks, but laughter stays,
In this garden, we'll sing our praise!

A Dance of Scarlet Dreams

In fields of red, the flowers sway,
With petals bright, they laugh and play.
A bumblebee trips, oh what a sight,
While butterflies giggle, taking flight.

They whisper jokes in the summer sun,
About the bees that try to run.
A ladybug winks, looking so grand,
As grasshoppers hop, forming a band.

The sunflowers wave like a tall parade,
While daisies twirl in a floral jade.
What a wacky time, this bloom-filled spree,
Where petals dance and all are free!

So come and join this funny sight,
Where colors blend in pure delight.
We'll laugh and spin till day is done,
In this garden full of silly fun!

Petals on the Gentle Breeze

Blowing softly on a gentle air,
Petals drift from here to there.
A sneaky breeze gives them a shove,
While flowers giggle, oh how they love!

They chase each other, round and round,
While daisies tumble on the ground.
A lilac smirks, its scent a tease,
As butterflies flutter with such ease.

A fidgety fern flaps with glee,
Wind whispers secrets, oh can't you see?
They all agree to join the chase,
A floral race, such a lively space!

Come take a spin on this plant-filled ride,
With nature's laughter as our guide.
We'll follow petals where they please,
Embracing joy on this little breeze!

Echoes of the Blooming Heart

In a garden where giggles bloom,
The flowers gossip, dispelling gloom.
A rose tells tales of love and cheer,
While violets chime in, oh so near.

The tulips boast of their vibrant hue,
While marigolds munch on leaves anew.
They share their dreams of the sun's warm light,
In a dance of colors, such a sight!

A cheeky bloom shouts, "Hey, come see,
The bees are buzzing just for me!"
They join the fun, with chatter and flair,
In a floral fiesta, beyond compare!

So gather round and lend your ear,
To the stories of joy and the laughter here.
In each petal's smile, a tale unfolds,
Of blooming hearts and laughter untold!

The Journey Through Painted Meadows

Through meadows bright, let's take a hop,
Where flowers giggle and never stop.
A butterfly slips on morning dew,
While daisies cheer, "We've waited for you!"

The sun paints rainbows across the field,
As nature's wonders are revealed.
A bouncing beetle tries to dance,
With twirling blossoms, oh what a chance!

The wind plays tunes on grass so green,
While blossoms bounce like a happy scene.
They sing of joy as they spin and twirl,
In this wild journey, let's give it a whirl!

So hop along with a smile so bright,
In these painted meadows, pure delight.
Each flower's laugh a melody sweet,
Join the journey where fun and flowers meet!

Fields of Ruby Whispers

In fields so bright, where colors play,
A cat in a hat danced all day.
He juggled bees, what a silly sight,
While frogs in bowties cheered with delight.

A chicken wearing sneakers took a chance,
With feathery flair, it joined the dance.
They twirled and tumbled, laughter flew,
In this wacky world where chaos grew.

Bumblebees buzzed with glee on the side,
As a squirrel in shades attempted to glide.
With nuts as his props, he put on a show,
And everybody watched, all aglow.

Fields of ruby, where laughter blooms,
And silliness brightens the fun-loving rooms.
Join in the frolic; don't miss the feast,
In this playful realm, joy's never ceased.

The Dance of Scarlet Blooms

In gardens grand, the flowers sway,
With petals bright, they laugh and play.
A gnome in sneakers, doing the twist,
Forget the rules, it's fun on the list!

Ladybugs chirp in a jazzy beat,
While butterflies flaunt their fanciful feet.
With flaps and flutters, they join the scene,
In a dance-off more silly than keen!

The daisies giggle, they can't stand still,
As worms in top hats make quite a thrill.
They cha-cha with roots, behind the grass,
Cheering each misstep, hoping for sass.

In this wild fiesta, joy takes flight,
As colors collide in pure delight.
With laughter resounding, all worries fade,
Let's join the dance; let's not be delayed!

Echoes in a Sea of Red

Across the fields where giggles flow,
A squirrel squeaked, 'Now, which way to go?'
He tried to surf on the wind's soft breeze,
And got tangled up in a cluster of trees!

A rabbit with shades was giving a tour,
While sunflowers clapped, they wanted more.
With carrots as snacks, they had a feast,
As clouds knocked, ready to join the beast.

A butterfly named Fred wore a funny hat,
And led the parade with a fat fluffy bat.
Together they giggled, embraced the red,
In a wacky world, they danced ahead.

So come and join this raucous spree,
Where laughter echoes, wild and free.
In a sea of colors, let's spin and twirl,
For the joy of this world is an unforgettable swirl.

A Journey Through Velvet Petals

On a road less traveled, oh what a sight,
A hedgehog on roller skates took flight.
With velvet petals paving the way,
He skidded and spun, oh a grand ballet!

A bear in pajamas shouted, "Yay!"
As flowers erupted in a bright cabaret.
They swayed in rhythm, feeling so groovy,
Embracing the weird, nothing felt too movie!

A duck with a trumpet tooted a tune,
Rallying bees beneath the full moon.
They honked and flapped, a funny parade,
While cactus dancers serenely swayed.

So let your heart wander, dance to the beat,
In this velvet paradise, we all can meet.
With joy as our guide, sing loud and clear,
For each silly moment is one we hold dear.

The Enchanted Blossom Route

On the road of blooms so bright,
Buzzing bees take wing in flight.
They dance and twirl, oh what a sight,
Sipping nectar, feeling light.

A ladybug dons a tiny hat,
Strutting 'round, imagine that!
With sunflower shades, oh how they chat,
While ants boast of their garden spat.

The butterflies wear their fanciest threads,
Complaining of the weight of their heads.
They flutter by with giggles and spreads,
In a world where laughter never dreads.

Join the parade, it's quite absurd,
Where every flower has the final word.
With petals squabbling, we've all heard,
In this realm, it's giggles that stirred.

Trails of the Sanguine Muse

On a trail paved with cherry cheer,
The rabbits gossip, lend an ear.
With carrot tales, they cause a sneer,
As they hop along, year after year.

A dandelion throws a wild spree,
Chasing clouds, oh so carefree!
While butterfly friends sip their tea,
In a garden buzzing in harmony.

The vivid blooms start a dance-off,
Kicking up petals with every scoff.
"Let's see your moves!" the daisies cough,
As laughter rings instead of scoff.

So sway along this merry track,
Where joy and folly don't hold back.
In a world where smiles are the knack,
Happiness follows right on the crack.

Scarlet Wandering Spirits

In the fields of laughter, spirits soar,
With tambourines and cheap decor.
They twirl in the air, oh what a bore,
Yet giggles bubble, they want more!

A mischievous gnome makes an appearance,
With mismatched socks, he prances in clearance.
Spilling seeds with wild joyous adherence,
Laughing loudly, no hint of a deference.

The flowers gossip, they start to sway,
Plotting antics to brighten the day.
"Who stole my pollen?" they play,
Laughter blooms in a quirky array.

So wander here, where spirits prance,
And every step invites a chance.
In this land of the silly dance,
Your worries cease, your heart entranced.

Pathways of Petal Dreams

Walk the lanes where petals fluff,
With breezy thoughts and laughter tough.
Where daisies discuss names of buff,
And tulips tease, "Ain't this enough?"

A butterfly fluffs a dramatic wing,
Playing diva, it makes us sing.
While grassy sprites begin to swing,
In a circus act of joyous bling.

A bumblebee with a royal grin,
Claims all the nectar, let's begin.
With honey jokes that twist and spin,
Watch out, for this won't be a sin!

So stroll along this jolly road,
Where wildflowers share the load.
In the realm of laughter flowed,
Every heart's joy will explode.

Delicate Steps on Fertile Ground

In a field where flowers play,
Bouncing bunnies hop all day.
With each foot that taps the earth,
They dance as if it's all their worth.

A clumsy crow takes flight with cheer,
And stumbles down, oh dear, oh dear!
With feathers fluffed, it strikes a pose,
Then off it goes, and who really knows?

A ladybug, all dressed in red,
Tries to recite some poems instead.
But each word rolls off her shell,
And giggles rise like a bubbling swell.

While beetles race on tiny bikes,
The laughter joins in giggling spikes.
In this patch where all is fun,
The soil's secrets are never done.

Embrace of the Crimson Horizon

In a glade where jokes bloom wide,
The sun is bold, it won't abide.
A squirrel cracks a nutty jest,
As birds in chorus join the fest.

A fox in shades, so sharply dressed,
Claims to be the very best.
The rabbits roll their eyes in jest,
"It's just a suit, so no, you're not blessed!"

A hedgehog spins in floral cap,
In every twirl, it takes a nap!
And while he snores, the flowers laugh,
"A prickly snooze? What a lovely gaffe!"

The sunset spills its orange hue,
As giggles tease the evening dew.
In this glow, the tales unwind,
A world where goofy dreams we find.

Spring's Sweet Revelations

Beneath the skies of swirling cheer,
The daisies shout, "Spring is here!"
With every sneeze, a flowers' style,
The bees all buzz and dance a while.

A worm in boots slips on the grass,
Declares, "I'm growing up, alas!"
But then it trips on leafy lace,
And rolls away without a trace.

Frogs hold court on lily pads,
In rhymes and jokes, they lose their fads.
One croaks a pun, the result is clear,
The cattails shake with laughter near.

As bumblebees in shades parade,
The flowers bellow, "Nice charade!"
In this spring of laughs galore,
The earth unveils her laughter's core.

Nature's Whispering Path

On winding trails where shadows play,
And whispers giggle in sun's ray.
A young deer stumbles, then it darts,
With antics full of merry hearts.

A curvy snail in funny shoes,
Claims it can dance, but it just snooze.
It twirls and spins, slow as can be,
"There's style in moving, wait for me!"

Within a thicket, the crickets sing,
With each chirp, they aim to fling.
Yet frogs on logs mock with some glee,
"Your concert's nice, but when's the spree?"

As trailblazers of mischief blend,
The faunas cheer, such fun to spend.
In nature's realm, where jesters meet,
The whispering path holds laughs so sweet.

A Tapestry of Red Shadows

In fields where giggles bloom,
The flowers dance with joy and loom.
A bee trips over petals bright,
Chasing dreams in morning light.

Bumbles bounce with silly grace,
Each step brings a laugh, a chase.
Red heads nod in gentle jest,
Nature's humor at its best.

A squirrel tries to wear a hat,
But it's far too small, oh what of that!
The flowers snicker, sway and sway,
As nature plays in bright display.

With every rustle, giggles grow,
In patches where the sunlight glows.
In this tapestry of hues so bold,
The funny tales of blooms unfold.

The Journey of Wildflower Echoes

Once a seed, so small and shy,
Dreamed of growing, reaching high.
But in the breeze it rolled away,
Fell in a garden where it could play.

It saw a daisy dressed in white,
Telling jokes of love at first sight.
The tulips giggled, whispered sweet,
As butterflies danced on tiny feet.

The blooms held a festival, you see,
With laughter and pollen confetti.
Amidst the wild and free-for-all,
They shared the joy, they shared the call.

In every petal, a story spun,
Of silly moments, laughter won.
The echoes of wildflower cheer,
Are memories that flourish here.

Veils of Vermilion Serenity

In a field awash with soft allure,
A ladybug finds that she's demure.
She struts along, a tiny queen,
Wearing polka dots for her routine.

The daisies gossip, petals curled,\nAbout the antics in their world.
"Have you heard what the clover said?
Something funny about a bear in red!"

A breeze kicks up with a cheeky swirl,
It tousles the ferns, gives them a twirl.
Their whispers meet the evening's bliss,
Laughing together, like this and this.

At dusk, the petals droop in mirth,
Exchanging jokes about their birth.
In veils of red and laughter free,
A serenade of joy's decree.

Walk Among the Crimson Waves

On a stroll through waves of ruby hue,
A rabbit hops, it's quite the view.
With every bounce, a teasing giggle,
He winks at foxes, making them wiggle.

The sun sets low, a chuckling glow,
As poppies sway, all in a row.
They whisper secrets to the breeze,
About the funny dances of bees.

With every step, the petals play,
Tickling toes that come their way.
Silly shadows flicker and tease,
This explosion of fun will never cease.

In the heart of crimson delight,
All creatures gather, day turns night.
A comedic parade, this joy enshrined,
In waves of laughter, forever intertwined.

Beneath the Canopy of Color

Underneath a rainbow sky,
Bumblebees buzz low and high.
Grasshoppers dance in silly ways,
While daisies giggle, caught in a haze.

The clouds wear hats that fit just right,
While squirrels put on quite the sight.
They jive with daisies, swing with glee,
Creating chaos, wild and free.

The sun tickles leaves with a bright grin,
As butterflies swirl, a colorful spin.
With every step, there's laughter ahead,
As flowers whisper jokes, widely spread.

Join this romp beneath the trees,
Where silly creatures do as they please.
Life's a jest in this blooming spree,
Come dance along, just you and me!

Dreams Weaved in Floral Threads

In dreamlands where the colors bloom,
Frogs wear pants, dispelling gloom.
They leap and bound with a croaky cheer,
Wearing crowns of daisies, without fear.

Butterflies debate with tiny ants,
On who can craft the best of dance.
Petals shout out quirky rhymes,
As ladybugs tap to funky chimes.

Sunshine whispers silly plots,
While ants gossip in flowery spots.
A trombone-wielding snail rocks the scene,
In this floral world, nothing's routine.

So dream along in this wacky space,
Where blooms abound and fun keeps pace.
With each twist and turn of leafy threads,
We weave our laughter where nature treads.

Crimson Trails of Memory

In fields where silly shadows play,
Crimson trails mark a jolly way.
Each step a story, each pause a jest,
As butterflies giggle, never at rest.

A rabbit hops in oversized shoes,
Chasing after a balloon, bright hues.
While trees wear grins and sway with glee,
As squirrels crack jokes, wild and free.

The breeze is a puppeteer, we know,
Tickling petals, putting on a show.
With every rustle, laughter is spun,
In this cheerful realm where we have fun.

Come trace the trails, forget your cares,
Join in the frolic, none can compare.
Memories painted in vermilion's hue,
Laughter's the art that we pursue.

Blossoms Beneath the Footsteps

Underfoot, the blossoms laugh,
As tiny critters take a bath.
The ground is soft, a cozy bed,
Where giggles sprout from every tread.

A hedgehog wears a tiny hat,
Waddling by with a silly spat.
Each bloom below shares tales of care,
As bees play tag in midair fair.

The mushrooms twirl and spin around,
As petals jump from the ground.
With each smile, the flowers bloom,
Creating joy, dispelling gloom.

So step with mirth, let laughter rise,
In this realm of colors and skies.
With every joyous step we take,
This blooming world, let's awake!

Secrets Hidden in Red Fields

In fields where the reds take the lead,
Ants march like soldiers, with no one to heed.
They gossip of treasures, both big and small,
While the breeze tells no secrets, it's having a ball.

A ladybug lounges, pretending to chat,
While grasshoppers leap, like a dance-off on that.
Bees bring sweet stories from flowers that bloom,
But can't share them well, for they're stuck in a zoom!

Little critters scurry, causing a stir,
Debating if nectar should rather be curry.
While daisies in laughter, they tickle the night,
And jest with the moon, unafraid of the fright.

If you stroll through the bloom, keep your secrets tight,
For the field will reveal every slip in your flight.
It's a wild roller coaster of colors and grace,
Just watch out for thorns when you pick up the pace!

The Lure of Floral Expedition

In a sea of bright colors, they beckon and tease,
Floral adventures, come take one, if you please.
With petals like whispers that giggle and sigh,
Each bloom holds a joke that's just waiting to fly.

A butterfly flutters, lost in a trance,
While bees are in therapy, discussing romance.
The daisies debate who's the fairest of all,
While tulips insist they're the life of the ball.

With sunshine as bottle and laughter as cork,
Every step is a giggle, a little firework.
Join in the revels, let the garden unwind,
For nature's concocted a potion, you'll find.

In the land of wild colors, all troubles should cease,
You'll leave with a grin and a sprinkle of peace.
So come grab your compass and don't forget cheer,
For each twist and turn brings new joys to appear!

Beneath the Blush of Sunset

The evening arrives, with a playful disguise,
As the sky turns to candy, igniting our eyes.
Whispers of laughter are painted with gold,
Every cloud has a story, just waiting to be told.

With fireflies dancing, both sparkly and bright,
And crickets composing a symphony of night.
The flowers all giggle, as colors collide,
Their petals are fluttering, full of sweet pride.

It's a circus of colors, and no one's afraid,
As shadows do cartwheels, this night is well-made.
So kick off your shoes, dance beneath the glow,
For beneath the blush, let your wild spirit flow.

With stardust and laughter, and joy in each breath,
We'll savor the sunset, defying the rest.
For life's but a canvas, and tonight it's a show,
Filled with secrets and dreams, let your true colors show!

Wanderlust in Fiery Hues

In fields of bright ribbons, where sunflowers grin,
We roam like lost children, where fun can begin.
With giggles and snickers, we bounce to and fro,
Each step is another online dance, don't you know?

The scarlet and orange sing songs of delight,
While tulips in clusters put up quite a fight.
They argue their shades in a colorful jest,
As bees serve as judges, in their pollen fest.

In a world full of colors, adventure awaits,
Where butterflies barter their cheese and their mates.
So join in the frolic, let your worries be few,
For where vibrant hues flourish, there's always a new.

With laughter the currency, we'll trade and we'll share,
In a realm where the flowers have stories to spare.
So wander this wonder, let your heart be so brave,
For in fiery hues, we'll dance upon waves!

Through the Loam of Petals

In fields where giggles bloom anew,
Bees wear tiny hats, it's true.
Bugs dance silly in the sun,
Their wobbly moves are just plain fun.

Twirling daffodils in bright array,
Laughing at clouds that drift away.
Silly shadows play tag with light,
Where sunbeams sparkle, oh what a sight!

A snail in boots plays hopscotch slow,
While butterflies gossip, flittering low.
A grasshopper leaps, with dreams to chase,
As daisies giggle in their green space.

So join the dance on this silly spree,
With petals soft as laughter, you'll see.
Nature's humor around every bend,
In fields of joy where giggles blend.

Hues of Forgotten Joy

Once in a garden, colors collide,
With shades of nostalgia, none can hide.
Lilies in socks, what a sight to behold,
Whispering secrets, daring and bold.

Crimson tomatoes sporting bright caps,
Planting their dreams in whimsical laps.
Zucchinis in bowties, looking so fine,
Share stories of yesteryears, oh how they shine!

Petunias in laughter, in pinks and in blues,
Swap tales of mischief, always amuse.
A daffodil winks, with a twinkle of cheer,
As laughter blooms brighter, the sun draws near.

In this garden of whimsy, joy takes its flight,
Colors of laughter spark day and night.
Join us in this dance of vibrant delight,
Where hues of merriment keep hearts light!

Traces of a Blazing Horizon

On a canvas stretched wide, the sun starts to play,
Painting the clouds in a rainbow ballet.
With every brushstroke, they giggle and spin,
As squirrels shake maracas for the fun to begin.

A rabbit in shades, sipping tea on the hill,
Cracks jokes with the sun, what a laugh, what a thrill!
The horizon, ablaze with a chortle or two,
As giggles roll over like morning dew.

Pigeons in sunglasses strut through the park,
Imitating funky dance moves after dark.
With a flip and a flap, they shuffle about,
Creating a ruckus, delight all throughout.

So let's tiptoe bravely, with giggles galore,
Chasing traces of joy, we'll forever explore.
In the blaze of the sunset, our laughter will rise,
A symphony bright under twilight skies.

The Call of Radiant Fragrance

In the air, there's a scent, quite funny indeed,
It tickles the nose, like a sweet little seed.
Roses in wigs, on a carnival ride,
Whisper tales of charm, no reason to hide.

Dandelions dressed like they're off to a ball,
Waving their fluff, answering the call.
With rhymes in the breeze, a frolicsome dance,
Each petal spins tales, giving hearts a chance.

Lemon balm giggles, faint breezy sighs,
While thyme and the mint share sweet little lies.
Lavender chuckles beneath a blue sky,
With fragrances lively, oh my, oh my!

So here's to the flowers with humor to lend,
In radiant scents, where laughter can blend.
Join the alchemy of fragrance and cheer,
With every whiff, let joy persevere!

Dreams Sketched in a Coral Bloom

In a garden where giggles sprout,
Petals tickle noses, there's no doubt.
Squirrels don hats, oh what a sight,
Dancing with bees in pure delight.

With each breeze, laughter's in the air,
Flowers gossip, like they really care.
A bunny's disco moves are grand,
While ants form bands, just like they planned.

Sunshine winks at every bee,
As butterflies join in, feeling free.
Dreams take flight on silly wings,
In this place, joy forever sings.

A rain cloud drifts, but not to frown,
It sprinkles giggles all around.
With puddles soft, our feet we splash,
In coral dreams, we dance and dash.

The Heartbeat of Flora's Domain

In Flora's realm, where colors play,
Butterflies chuckle the night away.
A flower thinks, maybe it should sing,
To the rhythm of bees, the joy they bring.

The daisies roll, quite out of line,
Telling jokes in a twisty vine.
While roses blush at stories told,
Of garden antics, both brave and bold.

Worms slither in a wiggly funk,
While petals bob, full of spunk.
A thistle spritzes jokes in the air,
As laughter mingles without a care.

From roots to blooms, the mirth does flow,
A vibrant scene, a laughing show.
In Flora's domain, the laughter's grand,
Where every bud has a playful hand.

Across the Swells of Rubies

Across the swells of red so bright,
Ladybugs sail through day and night.
With tiny caps, they steer the way,
On glimmers of laughter, they play.

A beetle performs a rollicking dance,
As roses giggle, offering a glance.
Petals polish their fanciful shoes,
While the sun beams down, showing off hues.

In this world of whimsical cheer,
Ants plot a parade, let's give a cheer!
With confetti made of bloom and dew,
Turning the ordinary into new.

The rubies sway with each silly prank,
In laughter's orchestra, they break rank.
Among the foliage, fun does swell,
In hues of laughter, all is well.

The Allurement of Flora's Palette

In Flora's palette, a scene so bright,
Tulips tell jokes till the fall of night.
With petals like paint, a canvas of glee,
Every bloom grinning, wild and free.

The violets chuckle, they twist and shout,
As daisies tumble, there's no doubt.
A sunflower ponders, what is the fun?
Maybe wearing shades under the sun!

Buttercups boast of their golden hue,
While giggling pansies join in too.
In shades of rich laughter, they bloom anew,
Creating a garden with humor so true.

As dusk descends on this cheerful space,
Fireflies twinkle, joining the race.
In Flora's palette, colors collide,
With nature's laughter, a joyful ride.

The Song of Quiet Gardens

In the garden, whispers flow,
Silly squirrels put on a show.
They dance around, with acorns in tow,
While grumpy cats steal the glow.

The roses giggle, petals twist,
Bumblebees join in with a twist.
Even the compost can't resist,
This garden's a party, can't be missed!

Twirling daisies, in bright array,
Worms are having a wild ballet.
Flowers chuckle, come what may,
Oh, what a jolly garden day!

In the shadows, secrets gleam,
Wandering through a flowery dream.
Sunflowers plot, or so it seems,
While fluttering leaves burst at the seams.

Shadows Dance on Floral Trails

Amidst the blooms, shadows prance,
Ladybugs join in for a chance.
They twirl and jig, what a romance,
While butterflies plot a new dance.

Rustling petals, giggles abound,
In every corner, laughter is found.
The evening stars gather 'round,
As crickets sing their funny sound.

Oh, the blooms with their comical style,
Bouncing around in the sun's smile.
They're hosting a gathering worthwhile,
With playful laughter, they beguile.

A bee in a hat, a bug in shoes,
Every creature has splendid views.
Together they share all the news,
In this garden, the funny muse.

Unfolding Roots of Resilience

Under the soil, mischief brews,
Roots intertwine, sharing some blues.
A funny tale of ancient dues,
As they wiggle, hiding their views.

The daisies giggle, gossiping well,
The orchids whisper, casting a spell.
Even the weeds have stories to tell,
Of overcoming and doing swell.

With every sprout, a laugh takes flight,
Sunshine tickles with all its might.
In this patch, everything feels right,
A comedic feast in the midday light.

The roots below, a tangled mess,
Yet thrive with joy, more or less.
In this dance, they won't confess,
Life's a joke, just take a guess!

The Elation of Blossoming Days

Laughter bursts as flowers wake,
Each bloom a joke, each petal a flake.
A sunflower winks, 'Oh, for goodness' sake!
While all the daisies giggle and shake.

They prance in the breeze with funny faces,
Butterflies join in, filling the spaces.
Our garden's alive with whimsical traces,
In every corner, joy embraces.

The bees chime in, singing a tune,
While clouds play peek-a-boo with the moon.
Life blooms in colors, bright as a cartoon,
Oh, the fun of spring afternoons!

Every bud unfolds with mirthful glee,
As nature crafts its own jubilee.
In this patch of laughter, wild and free,
Every blossom is a comedy spree!

The Warm Embrace of Autumn's Hues

Leaves tumble down, oh what a sight,
Wearing jackets, they dance in flight.
Chasing squirrels with acorn caps,
Nature giggles, the world adapts.

Sunshine winks through branches bare,
Pumpkin spice fills the crisp, cool air.
Sipping cider, we laugh and cheer,
Autumn's quirks bring us all near.

Sweaters hugging, a snug delight,
Raccoons rummage in the moonlight.
A parade of colors, crowds the scene,
With every crunch, we feel like teens.

Sprinkling laughter, like leaves they twirl,
This season's charm makes hearts unfurl.
Jokes are shared with friends so dear,
Autumn's warmth, let's shed a tear!

Veils of Radial Petal Light

In gardens bright, the flowers mock,
Spinning tales 'round the old clock.
Bees in bowties buzz with flair,
While Ladybugs steal the fair share.

Sunlight dances on each petal's face,
Bumbling butterflies join the race.
Chasing shadows, they flirt and glide,
Nature's laughter cannot hide.

Daisies tease with a playful bend,
"Catch us if you can!" they send.
With petals fluffed and colors bold,
The garden's a circus, a sight to behold.

The wind whispers secrets, oh what a show,
A budding romance with each flower's glow.
Laughter blooms where the colors ignite,
In this wild world of floral delight.

The Enchantment of the Flowered Road

Down the lane, where blooms all meet,
Stumbling flowers dance on their feet.
With hats askew, they sway and play,
Every step's a bright bouquet!

Bumblebees wearing fuzzy shoes,
Bip-bopping to nature's news.
With every step, they tickle our toes,
While petals giggle as the spring wind blows.

Each blossom boasts a sunny grin,
In this floral realm, we just can't win.
They twirl and whirl like they own the show,
While we just wander, moving slow.

Joy blooms larger as we tread on,
With every bloom, a new yarn spun.
This path of petals, we can't resist,
Nature's laughter, oh, we persist!

Trails of Light Among Petal Shadows

In gardens where shadows play and tease,
We chase the sun, oh what a breeze!
With flowers' whispers, secrets loud,
We frolic under a sunlit cloud.

Dandelions laugh and wiggle near,
Pretending to be tough, we cheer.
But when the wind gives them a nudge,
Their poofing seeds make us begrudge!

The lilacs sigh and roll their eyes,
While tulips plot their surprise prize.
Whimsical petals dance around,
A flower party, so profound.

With trails of light that flicker bright,
And petals laughing, oh what a sight!
Through these blooms, we stumble on,
In nature's jig, we're never gone!

Entranced by Nature's Warmth

In fields of red, we trot and play,
With flowers dancing, what a ballet!
They wave their heads, we laugh and spin,
Nature's joke, where do we begin?

The bees are buzzing, a silly hum,
They zoom around, oh where are they from?
We chase their tails, but they just buzz,
In this sweet chaos, oh how we fuzz!

The sunbeams giggle, slipping through,
Tickling our noses, a warm debut.
With petals swirling like hats in flight,
We're merry fools, embracing delight!

So here we dance in our floral spree,
With laughter echoing, wild and free.
Each bloom a joker in nature's act,
In this bright world, we're fully packed!

The Odyssey of Swaying Stems

Once upon a time, in fields so wide,
Stems wiggled and wobbled, a comical ride!
The clumsy wind made grass do the twist,
Who knew a breeze could be such a tryst?

A dance-off started, oh what a sight,
With daisies and daisies, twirling with might.
A tulip stumbled, fell to the ground,
"Oh dear!" it shouted, "How awkward, I'm bound!"

The dandelions chuckled, blowing their fluff,
"We're the kings of chaos, isn't that enough?"
Their laughter echoed, a riotous cheer,
In this tall grass stage, full of zany cheer.

So here they sway, with roots so tight,
Natural pratfalls, oh what pure delight!
In this merry romp, there's magic in air,
Swaying stems giggle, they haven't a care!

The Allure of Flowered Ridges

Up on the hill, where colors collide,
Flowers in hats, they stroll with pride.
A daffodil tripped, stumbled headlong,
"You'd think I'd learned, but I still sing wrong!"

The butterflies laughed, in flutters so grand,
With wings painted bright, they took to the land.
They teased the petals, who knew they could fly,
"Join our parade, come twirl in the sky!"

A rose in a wink, said, "I'm quite the catch,
With perfume so sweet, I'll make quite the match!"
Next to the daisies, all giggly and bright,
Together they danced, oh what a sight!

And as the sun sets, they laugh and beam,
In their flowered realm, every whim is a dream.
They twirl and they sway, in hues of delight,
These ridges of laughter, a pure delight!

Trails of Blazing Inspiration

On trails ablaze, with colors so bold,
We prance through blooms, like stories told.
With flowers a-chatter, in shades that shine,
"Who wore it better? This hat or mine?"

The bees are the judges, buzzing with glee,
"Dear petals, we follow your match for a spree!"
Giggling petals, in rustling rows,
Together they bloom, and whimsically pose!

A butterfly laughed, "I've got some flair,
In my polka-dot wings, catch me if you dare!"
They zoomed like arrows, with cracks of delight,
In this fragrant race, pure joy takes flight!

So onward we wander, through colorful dreams,
With trails of laughter, and sunshine beams.
In a world so lively, full of surprises,
Each step we take, laughter never disguises!

Wandering Through Cotton Candy Clouds

In a sky made of sugary strands,
I dance on sweet cotton bands.
With a giggle, I float and sway,
As the marshmallow sun leads the way.

Lollipop trees line the bright route,
With candy cane roots, oh what a hoot!
I chase a licorice breeze that sings,
A tune that only sugar can bring.

As gummy bears join in the fun,
We skip along 'til the day is done.
With each bounce, the giggles grow loud,
In this land of whimsy, I'll stand proud!

And when the day bids soft goodbye,
I'll dream of candy clouds up high.
With sweet adventures in store for me,
I'll wander through joy, wild and free!

The Language of Quiet Petals

Whispers float on petals anew,
Each bloom tells a story or two.
A daisy with a cheeky grin,
Winks at the grass, oh where to begin?

A tulip shimmies, bright in the sun,
Says, 'Dance a bit, let's have some fun!'
With petals that giggle in the breeze,
They spread laughter like the sweetest tease.

Roses boast in colors so bold,
Sharing secrets, both new and old.
A flower dance-offs near the gate,
Making pollen partners—oh, what a fate!

In this floral chatter, so sweet,
Every bloom knows how to compete.
With humor and charm they take their stand,
In the garden, it's all quite grand!

Tapestry of Nature's Palette

Brushstrokes of green in the park,
With splashes of yellow where squirrels embark.
Crimson leaves flutter like a mad kite,
Creating a quilt, oh what a sight!

Violet berries giggle on trees,
While daisies chuckle beneath the bees.
A path paved with laughter, what a delight,
Nature bursts forth in pure, merry flight!

With twirling dandelions, I blow a wish,
A jabbering brook sings a fishy swish.
An orchestra played by chirping and croaks,
With nature's humor in all its strokes.

So come take a peek at the grand display,
Where every leaf has something to say.
A vibrant show, where colors sing,
In this tapestry, let happiness spring!

Trails of Earth and Bloom

On trails where earth and dreams collide,
Flowers giggle and joy won't hide.
The path's a dance of petal and seed,
Each step a laugh, a whimsical deed!

With a hop and a skip through the green,
Charms of nature laugh, light, and keen.
Wandering critters join my spree,
In this playful world where we are free!

Bubbly brooks play tag with the sun,
As flowers sway, they know how to run.
A tickle of grass beneath my toes,
Sends laughter echoing where laughter flows.

So let's wander these magical trails,
Where giggles echo and joy prevails.
With each step taken, we celebrate cheer,
In this garden of laughter, we hold dear!

Immersed in Nature's Crimson

In fields where clowns and flowers dance,
The bees wear hats, they take a chance.
A ladybug plays peek-a-boo,
While grasshoppers jump in their bright green shoe.

With every step, a squishy sound,
Are those my shoes or the mud I've found?
A butterfly flutters, wearing a tie,
Saying, 'Time to party!' as he zooms by.

Amidst the laughter, a squirrel jests,
Collecting acorns for his wild quests.
"Hey, you!" he chortles, "Want to race?
I'll even let you borrow my face!"

Sunshine paints the world quite bright,
As joyous critters share delight.
Nature's banquet, with snacks galore,
Who knew the outdoors could be such a chore?

Melodies of Wildflower Lullabies

The daisies hum a silly tune,
While daisies twirl, beneath the moon.
A rabbit croons a lullaby,
While starlit frogs sing, oh so spry.

A dandelion blew a kiss,
To a butterfly, who couldn't resist.
They flit and flutter, up in the air,
Spreading joys without a care.

Crickets play their tiny drums,
As sleepy ants just twiddle thumbs.
"Let's hit the hay," a bumblebee grins,
While sleepy blooms wear sleepy spins.

As night falls gently, a tint of cheer,
The moon giggles, "What's that I hear?"
Nature's symphony is a riot,
Come join the fun, don't be quiet!

Cascades of Blushing Petals

In gardens where colors collide,
Petals tumble down the slide.
A beetle dressed up all in gold,
Says, "What's next? A rock and roll!"

With bursts of laughter in the air,
The blooms giggle without a care.
A snail zooms past, lacking speed,
"Am I too slow? I might concede!"

Fluffy clouds perform acrobatics,
While squirrels act out athletic tactics.
"Catch me if you can!" they tease and dash,
Taking off in a wild flash!

Each petal sparkles in delight,
As the sun winks goodnight.
In this garden, life's a jest,
Join in, dear friend, it's for the best!

Summer's Reddest Romance

The sun blushes as it begins to flirt,
With berries wearing their finest shirt.
A frog croaks out a cheesy line,
"Cute ladybug, wanna dine?"

The roses giggle and sway in glee,
As butterflies sip on sweet iced tea.
"Your wings look ravishing!" one will say,
Turning meadow into a cabaret!

Sunflowers nod at every joke,
While bees buzz by with a cheerful poke.
"Love is in the air," a bumblebee sighs,
With hearts and flowers in their eyes.

As the day fades with a wink and grin,
Summer wraps all in a merry spin.
Nature's love fest fills the air,
Come join the fun, if you dare!

Where the Sun Meets the Blossom

In fields where flowers dance and twirl,
Bees in bow ties make quite the whirl.
A sunflower wears a goofy grin,
While daisies chuckle, 'Where to begin?'

The sunlight splashes like spilled paint,
A lazy caterpillar draws faint.
Sipping nectar, with a wink and a squint,
Life here is silly, and that's no hint!

Secrets of the Verdant Road

On a road where laughter blooms and spills,
Chickens in hats have their quirky thrills.
A hedgehog juggles odd-shaped stones,
While crickets play tunes, in silly tones.

Trees whisper secrets, oh, what a jest!
A squirrel in sneakers claims he's the best.
But watch your step, or you might just fall,
Into a patch where grass makes the call!

Labyrinth of Vibrant Hues

In a maze of colors so bright and bold,
A turtle in shades thinks he's pure gold.
Butterflies waltz with a quirky flair,
While laughing flowers tickle the air.

Dandelions plot behind sneaky tall grass,
Winking at blooms as they wiggle and sass.
Come join the fun in this garden spree,
Where giggles grow wild, as wild as can be!

A Wayward Path of Wildflowers

Down the path where wild blooms play,
A fox in socks leads the way, hooray!
The wind tells jokes only daisies hear,
While toadstools laugh at a clueless deer.

A rambunctious breeze tussles each stem,
As butterflies dress in fashion's gem.
Join the parade of nature's delight,
Where every step brings a giggle in sight!

Symphony of Scarlet Fields

In fields where flowers play hide and seek,
A squirrel serenades with a squeaky peak.
The daisies giggle, the wind starts to dance,
While bees pull pranks in a floral romance.

The sun brings laughter, a jovial cheer,
As ladybugs waltz with no hint of fear.
Ants in a conga line march to the beat,
Of nature's jokes on this whimsical street.

A butterfly trips on a leaf of delight,
Flapping its wings in a comical flight.
The flowers, like jesters, bow with a grin,
Promising troubles will never begin.

So if you wander through this floral domain,
Join in the laughter; it's pleasure, not pain.
For in every petal lies a world of giggles,
On the canvas of nature where happiness wiggles.

Echoes of Floral Radiance

In gardens where wild colors shout,
Sunflowers play peekaboo all about.
The tulips gossip in whispers so sweet,
In a waltz of colors, they tap their neat feet.

Dandelions puff with a proud little strut,
While butterflies tease in their pastel cut.
Snails have their races, but all take their time,
With jokes so old they must be a rhyme.

The breeze carries giggles, a playful wind,
As blooms break into laughter, their laughter rescinds.
A caterpillar dreams of a grand parade,
While daisies wink at the sunshine's cascade.

So pause for a moment, let the joy ye reap,
Among floral echoes where laughter takes leap.
For every flower sings a tune so divine,
In a chorus of giggles, all troubles resign.

The Path to Floral Reverie

On a winding trail through colors galore,
Flowers tell tales that you can't ignore.
Each petal a story, a giggle, a sigh,
With blooms all around, it's a colorful sky.

A bee with a bowtie buzzes with flair,
While roses play dress-up, with perfume to spare.
The path twists and turns like a comical sketch,
As daisies line up for their evening fetch.

Butterflies tease in their fluttering spree,
Dancing around, saying, "Come join with me!"
A crow makes a joke; the sun starts to set,
In laughter and blooms, there's no room for regret.

So wander this pathway, with laughter in store,
In a dream of bright colors, who could ask for more?
For every step taken is a giggle bestowed,
On this journey through wonder, where joy overflowed.

Dance of Vibrant Blossoms

Under the sunshine, flowers frolic and leap,
With petals like skirts, they twirl in a heap.
A tulip does cartwheels, a daisy will spin,
As laughter erupts from each floral grin.

In the center, a foxglove leads with a cheer,
As bees form a circle, all buzzing near.
The daisies roll over, tickled by grass,
While violets laugh, letting good moments pass.

A humorous wind pulls the flowers along,
Each petal a note in a joyous song.
Lilies are gossiping under the sun,
Trading their secrets about how they've won.

At dusk, when the colors begin to fade,
The flowers exchange their last joyous trade.
For in every dance, there's a smile to keep,
On this hilarious journey, where laughter runs deep.

Celestial Whispers

The moon forgot its cheese tonight,
A comet stole a bite with glee.
Stars giggled, twinkling with delight,
While planets danced in cosmic spree.

Jupiter's full of orange jokes,
Saturn spins with rings of fun.
Mars teases with its dusty cloaks,
While Venus shines, a fiery one.

Original title:
Planetary Prose

Copyright © 2025 Creative Arts Management OÜ
All rights reserved.

Author: Vivienne Beaumont
ISBN HARDBACK: 978-1-80567-770-3
ISBN PAPERBACK: 978-1-80567-891-5

Orbiting Dreams

In dreams, I float on stardust streams,
With aliens who love to skydive.
They wear bright hats and giggle gleams,
As we all orbit and jive.

Uranus rolls with laughter loud,
Pluto pouts, feeling out of place.
We build a goofy, joyful crowd,
In this vast, spinning, starry space.

The Language of Stars

Stars whisper puns in the twilight,
While black holes laugh, they can't pull in.
Constellations play hide and seek,
As meteors zoom, what a din!

Saturn's rings, a hula hoop,
Galaxies swirl in a dizzy dance.
Neptune joins the cosmic troop,
Catching starlight with a glance.

Beyond the Cosmic Veil

Beyond the veil of dark and light,
Aliens bake space cookies bright.
The sun plays peekaboo with night,
As stars perform in cosmic sight.

Cosmic dust gets into their eyes,
They chuckle at the swirling show.
Finding joy in starlit skies,
As comets laugh and merrily flow.

Starbound Verses

In a rocket that farts,
We zoom past the stars.
Lunchtime in zero G,
My sandwich floats far.

Alien ads sing,
For zany space snacks.
With flavors like pickle,
And moon cheese, oh, yacks!

Mars yawns in the night,
While Venus spills tea.
Jupiter's cranky,
His storms just won't flee.

Yet on this wild trip,
A laugh is the best.
Among cosmic weirdos,
We share our strange jest.

The Language of Galaxies

Stars gossip with flair,
In a cosmic café.
They sip on stardust,
And banter all day.

Black holes tell tall tales,
Of things they have gobbled.
While comets do flips,
As the earthlings just hobbled.

Supernovae pop,
Like fireworks grand.
They celebrate life,
With a space marching band.

In this universe vast,
Laughter's our guide.
For in the expanse,
We'll forever abide.

Twilight Reveries

The sun winks goodnight,
As the stars come to play.
The moon pulls up chairs,
For a galactic buffet.

Nebulas giggle,
In colors so bright.
They play hide and seek,
Till the fall of the night.

Asteroids dance by,
To a raucous parade.
While space-time falls flat,
On an interstellar charade.

What stories they weave,
In the twilight's embrace.
Funny dreams abound,
In this vast, goofy space.

Dreams from the Dark Side of the Moon

In shadows, we plot,
With laughter and schemes.
The moon's darkened face,
Holds our silliest dreams.

Tidal waves of glee,
Roll on lunar shores.
As craters hum tunes,
On invisible boars.

Astronauts trip up,
In their clunky space boots.
While aliens laugh,
In their one-eyed suits.

But underneath stars,
In this night that's so vast,
We find fun together,
In dreams meant to last.

Cosmic Parables

In a galaxy far, so they say,
Aliens laugh in a most silly way.
They knit their socks with stardust threads,
And tell tall tales of moonlit beds.

On Jupiter's breeze, a rumble and giggle,
A worm spins tales that make us wiggle.
In cosmic cafes, they sip space juice,
Sharing jokes that leave us quite loose.

Horizons Beyond

Beyond the stars, where the llamas roam,
A comet dances, calling each home.
With Saturn's rings made of candy cane,
The sweet tooth fairies play a game.

The sun wears shades, oh what a sight,
While Earth's got its dance moves just right.
In the Nebula Night, they twirl and spin,
The laughter echoes, let the fun begin!

The Orbit of Thoughts

In circles, our ideas go round and round,
Like a dog in a chase, lost but found.
A thought shoots past like a shooting star,
"Did I turn the oven off?" Wonder afar.

Galaxies swirl in a silly parade,
Where confusion reigns, but never fades.
We think of snacks while in cosmic chat,
As black holes giggle, "Now, what's up with that?"

Whispers from the Void

In the deepness, someone softly snorts,
A laugh from nowhere, in space it cavorts.
Ghosts of comets leave trails of glee,
While asteroids roll by shouting, 'Whee!'

The void whispers secrets, quite outrageous,
Of distant worlds, all preposterous.
Wormholes chuckle at cosmic pranks,
As we spin in circles, filling our tanks.

Echoes in the Galaxy

In a rocket made of cheese,
Aliens dance with utmost ease.
They juggle stars and sip on sun,
Laughing as they have their fun.

Asteroids roll like bowling balls,
While Martians paint their cosmic walls.
A comet sneezes, and oh dear me,
It sneezes out a rainbow spree.

Terrestrial Sonnet

Down on Earth, the cows complain,
While frogs in suits play chess in rain.
The trees hold meetings, quite absurd,
Debating loudly, not one word heard.

A snail in boots runs to the show,
While worms put on their best tango.
The bugs all tap in harmony,
Creating quite the symphony.

Celestials in Dusk

Stars in pajamas, oh what a sight,
Throwing pillows in a cosmic fight.
The moon laughs loudly, glowing bright,
As meteors tumble, what a night!

Planets wear hats, so out of style,
Saturn's rings dance with a smile.
While Venus winks with a cheeky glow,
And Neptune's sipping on spacey flow.

Harmonies of the Universe

In galaxies where giggles reign,
Galactic whales sing sweet refrains.
Uranus twirls in rhythm fine,
While Pluto scribbles a wild line.

Quasars flicker, each note a delight,
With echoes bouncing through the night.
Cosmic clowns juggle comets high,
Making every star burst out with a sigh.

The Sound of Silence in Space

In the void, I hear a sneeze,
Asteroids giggle, what a tease!
Neptune's got a mighty cold,
Yelling constellations, bold and old.

The stars all whisper, 'Take a break!'
But I'm too busy for a cake.
A comet jokes, 'Got room for me?'
And I just laugh, floating carefree.

Wandering Between Stars

I strolled through a void, quite bizarre,
Tripped over Saturn's rings—oh, dear, a star!
Venus winked, said, 'Try my pie!'
But it's baked in a nebula, oh my!

Uranus rolled by in a laughter spree,
Said, 'Some say I'm rude, but I'm just free!'
Between giggles, I made my way,
Astroids throwing a dance party, hooray!

The Unknown at Light Speed

Zooming fast, a flash of light,
Speeding past a black hole's bite.
What's that? A sock all alone!
Did it slip from a comet's throne?

Planets turn their heads and gawk,
Mars taught me how to moonwalk.
In a race, I lost my lunch,
But who knew stars could pack a punch?

Journal of a Wandering Astronomer

Entry one: I lost my hat,
To a passing meteor, imagine that!
Wrote to Venus for a new look,
But she only sent me a strange book.

Day three: I tripped on a moonbeam,
All the galaxies laughed, what a scene!
I asked the sun, 'Why so bright?'
He said, 'To light your silly flight!'

Rhythms of the Night Sky

The moon danced like a silly clown,
While stars wore hats that fell right down.
They twirled and twisted, all in jest,
Creating rhythms that never rest.

A meteor zoomed, a cosmic race,
But tripped on Saturn's rings, what a place!
Jupiter laughed, a giant balloon,
As comets threw confetti in the afternoon.

A shooting star fell, 'Oops, that was close!'
While Earth sighed, 'Just another cosmic dose.'
Galaxies chuckled with dazzling flair,
In the silly ballroom of the midnight air.

The Constellation of My Mind

In my brain, stars flash and blink,
Ideas colliding, faster than you think.
Orion's belt is my to-do list,
But forget it often, like an angry fist.

Pisces swim in circles, what a scene,
Making waves in thoughts, so serene.
While Leo roars for snacks, oh dear,
The snack star's orbit is very near.

I chart my dreams on a napkin or two,
With scribbles of planets that no one knew.
My cosmos spins in a glorious mess,
Creating laughter, I must confess.

Lights in the Abyss

Out in the cosmos, where shadows play,
Lights flicker like they're here to stay.
A neon comet blinks, 'Check me out!'
But the black hole just glares with a pout.

Stars wink from the void, doing silly tricks,
While aliens groove to their funky mix.
A supernova burst had them in stitches,
As cosmic dust settled, oh what glitches!

The void chuckled softly, 'Can't take a break!'
As quasar jokes launched, like cakes from a lake.
In the abyss, joy breaks through the dark,
With every twinkle, a jolly spark.

The Unwritten Map of Stars

Oh, the stars scribble sketches on space,
Naughty constellations, they just race!
The map's all crooked, and lines go askew,
With arrows pointing to places anew.

Galactic scribblers scatter bright ink,
While I sit confused, far on the brink.
X marks the spot, but it's lost, I fear,
In endless giggles, stars plot, cheer!

A star tried to draw my dream vacation,
But it landed on Mars—what a sensation!
With laughter erupting in every curve,
The map of the stars knows how to swerve.

The Gravity of Words

Words drift like planets,
Spinning tales of glee,
A comet's tail of laughter,
Makes space feel so free.

Floating on hot air,
Jokes collide and burst,
In a black hole of puns,
Where we all quench our thirst.

Gravity pulls at my sides,
As I giggle and pray,
For the cosmic humor,
To light up my day.

So grab your space boots,
Let's bounce to the beat,
In a universe of jests,
Where nothing's too sweet.

Whispers from the Void

In the silence of space,
Laughter echoes clear,
Alien jokes abound,
Who knew they'd be here?

Stars chat about life,
In a cosmic café,
Sipping sunbeam smoothies,
In a funny old way.

Nebulas giggle softly,
While black holes yawn wide,
Saying, "We're all just dust,
On this wild joyride!"

So join the laughter,
High above the ground,
In the whispers of void,
Funny friendship is found.

Orbits of Time

Time spins in circles,
Wobbling like a top,
With seconds doing salsa,
As the tick-tock won't stop.

Minutes wear pajamas,
As they dance through the air,
While hours play hide and seek,
Without a single care.

Days juggle their duties,
Winking from afar,
As weeks tilt their hats,
Like they're at a bazaar.

So let's twirl with time,
In this comedic race,
For in each merry orbit,
We find joy in our pace.

Milky Way Melodies

Underneath the stars,
A band starts to play,
With planets on drums,
And moons in ballet.

Asteroids dance wildly,
To a rhythm so rare,
While comets sing softly,
Like they just don't care.

Galaxies harmonize,
In a cosmic parade,
With laughs twirling round,
In this vast serenade.

So let's sway in starlight,
On a laugh-filled spree,
With Milky Way melodies,
That tickle the spree.

The Musing Cosmos

In a galaxy far, far away,
Stars giggle at the Milky Way.
Planets dance, in bright tutus,
Making space dust with their shoes.

Asteroids with donuts in hand,
Orbiting near a glittering band.
Jupiter's jealous of all the style,
While Saturn just spins with a smile.

Neptune's getting a makeover today,
With cosmic hair in a bright array.
Mars likes to boast of its red hue,
But Venus says, "I'm way cuter too!"

Black holes laughing, pulling in light,
"Not so fast!" they tease in delight.
The sun tells jokes that are hot and bright,
While comets swoosh past in the night.

Vibrations of Eternity

There's a rhythm in the sky so vast,
Galaxies twirl, having a blast.
Stars are jamming to a cosmic tune,
While aliens brazenly dance in June.

Mars bumps along in its clay-like shoes,
While Earth trades barbs on the latest news.
Saturn's rings are a hula-hoop craze,
As planets groove in their own funny ways.

Wormholes pop with a snicker and grin,
"Come on through! Where should we begin?"
Shooting stars shoot right past the moon,
Singing their wishes with a cheeky tune.

Black holes spin like it's party time,
Pulling in jokes that rhyme and chime.
The universe winks, we all have a laugh,
In this cosmic jest, let's share a gaffe.

Celestial Whispers

In the night sky, whispers pass by,
Stars gossip endlessly, oh my!
The moon rolls its eyes, in silver delight,
While comets compete for the best flight.

Uranus chuckles, it's tilted just so,
Says, "I'm the best, just look at my glow!"
But Pluto just winks, oh what a sport,
"I'm still a planet in this funny court."

Galaxies chat with a twinkling flair,
Spilling secrets of love in the air.
Supernovas yell, "Look at me shine!"
While black holes wink, saying "You can't dine!"

Every star in this infinite jest,
Shares a giggle, feeling quite blessed.
The cosmos plays games, it's a cosmic mall,
Where laughter and light are the best of all.

Echoes of the Cosmos

Echoes ring through the infinite space,
Planets jive in a zealous race.
Shooting stars shout with cosmic cheer,
"Hey, Earth! We brought you this year!"

On Mercury, they play a fast-paced game,
As Venus rolls dice, calling out names.
Jupiter's belly bursts forth in glee,
With every tickle of cosmic spree.

Neptune's whispers, "Pass the space cake,"
While Saturn's rings make jokes that break.
Black holes snicker, "A vacuum's our style,
So suck it up—we're here for a while!"

Through the echoes, laughter expands,
Bouncing around under starlit bands.
In this universe where whimsy prevails,
The cosmos erupts in jubilant tales.

Celestial Dreams

In a galaxy, far and wide,
Aliens giggle, they cannot hide.
Moonbeams tickle their strange toes,
While asteroids dance in fancy clothes.

Stars wear hats, so very bright,
They party hard all through the night.
Cosmic cakes with frosting glow,
And black holes serve as seats, you know.

Comets race with ice cream cones,
Playing tag with cosmic drones.
While Saturn spins like a disco ball,
They twirl around, having a ball.

In this place where fun is king,
Laughter echoes, a joyful thing.
Planets trade their dusty gear,
For soap bubbles that float near.

The Secret Life of Comets

Comets whizzing, tails all aflame,
Secret pranks are their favorite game.
They slip on ice, and slide on by,
While giggling like kids in a pie.

Each one wears a sparkling dress,
Filled with stardust, no less, no less!
They swoop and dive, shout, "Catch me now!"
As planets look with awe, oh wow!

In ice cream trucks, they zip and zoom,
Deliver treats to the lunar room.
Flavors like stardust, cosmic swirls,
While moons laugh and dance, little girls and pearls.

They wink at Mars while flipping a coin,
Hoping it's the Earth that they'll join.
With cosmic mischief filling the sky,
Those comet kids always fly high.

Luminescent Poems of the Universe

In starlit ease, the verses glow,
Words float softly, to and fro.
A nebula's giggle, a sunbeam's cheer,
Happiness lingers, oh so near.

Planets whisper jokes in the breeze,
As shooting stars dance with such ease.
Galaxies swirl in a humorous jest,
Each quasar laughing, feeling blessed.

The asteroids chuckle, they roll and tumble,
Creating rhymes that never stumble.
With vses wrapped in twinkling light,
The universe beams with pure delight.

In the cosmic swirl, laughter flows,
As poems bloom where starlight glows.
Each word, a twirl, a shimmering thread,
Weaving stories of laughter, joy widespread.

Shimmering Thoughts from Beyond

In the realm where shooting stars race,
Thoughts shimmer softly, full of grace.
Galaxies gossip with a giggle or two,
While black holes hum a merry tune.

Venus wears spectacles, looking quite smart,
Jupiter's dancing, a wobbly art.
Lightyears away, they trade silly dreams,
In this cosmic spree, all's not as it seems.

Nebulas laugh, their colors all bright,
Painting the skies with a joyful delight.
Uranus spins, joking with flair,
While Saturn tosses rings in the air.

Here in the cosmos, joy takes flight,
With each twinkling star, everything's right.
Shimmering thoughts weave a tapestry fine,
In the laughter of space, all souls intertwine.

Cosmic Tapestries

In the universe so vast and wide,
Aliens dance with galactic pride.
They wear sombreros and big shoes too,
While sipping drinks of cosmic dew.

Stars play hide and seek at night,
As comets zoom with all their might.
Planets giggle when they collide,
Creating rings that swirl with pride.

A sunbeam tickles a moonlit face,
Sending silly shadows to outer space.
They laugh at asteroids' silly strut,
As they twist and turn in a cosmic rut.

So grab your rocket, let's take flight,
Through all the giggles of starlit night.
The universe is a cosmic jest,
With laughter echoing in the quest.

Fragments of Starlight

Twinkle twinkle, little star,
Did you just fall in from afar?
Maybe tripped on a cosmic ray,
Or slipped on moonbeams gone astray.

Each fragment tells a funny tale,
Of space-faring cows in a sunny gale.
They moo-ed their way through the Milky sea,
With astronaut hats, oh so carefree!

Funny planets spin in disguise,
With googly eyes and silly ties.
They dance around the asteroid belt,
In a silly jig that's truly felt.

So when you gaze at the night's array,
Just know the cosmos is here to play.
In every twinkle, in every beam,
There's laughter bursting at the seams.

Mysteries of the Milky Way

In the spiral arms of a chocolate swirl,
Galactic frogs jump and twirl.
They croak the secrets of time and space,
While wearing sunglasses with style and grace.

Planets gossip on their merry way,
Trading jokes in the light of day.
A comet moves with a wobbly stride,
Waving 'hello' with an icy slide.

Shooting stars with jokes to share,
Sprinkle wishes in the cosmic air.
You might just find a witty gem,
In the vastness of this galactic hem.

So grab a seat, and join the show,
Where the universe busts a rhyme or two.
Laughter echoes from here to Mars,
A celestial comedy written in stars.

The Wandering Comet's Tale

A comet wanders with a gleeful grin,
Painting the sky with sparkles of sin.
It stops to chat with the planets round,
Sharing laughs that know no bound.

'Twas here I saw a space cow play,
Riding a meteor on its way!
With a lasso twinkling bright in the night,
Catching giggles that took flight.

Its tail a swirl of bright confetti,
It twirls around like it's all so petty.
Stars shake their heads at its silly spree,
Wondering how wild this space could be.

So if you see it streaking by,
Join in the fun, don't be shy!
Wandering comets weave tales so bright,
In the endless laughter of the night.

Constellation Conundrums

In the sky, stars twist and twirl,
Where the big dipper gives a whirl.
Orion's belt seems quite the tale,
Is that a hunter or a snail?

Shooting stars, they often blink,
Wishing well, or just a wink?
Pegasus flies, oh what a sight,
But trip over clouds, what a fright!

Ursa Major starts to snore,
While Cassiopeia's checking score.
Celestial pets in their own delight,
Doggos barking at meteors tonight!

Comets dance with tails so bright,
Waving hello as they take flight.
Stargazers scratch their puzzled heads,
Is that a star or bun on bread?

Astrological Musings

Oh dear Taurus, please don't charge,
Your stubborn ways are quite too large.
Gemini plays tag with the moon,
While Leo howls his favorite tune.

Libra's scales are far from straight,
Weighing chocolate on a plate.
Scorpio hides in shadows and shrieks,
Spilling secrets in the creeks.

Sagittarius bows and shoots,
Missing targets, tying boots.
Capricorn counts the stars above,
While Aquarius waves with love!

Pisces dreams in a fishy fashion,
Swimming through galaxies with passion.
And Virgo checks her to-do list,
Stars can wait; she insists!

The Rhythm of the Spheres

Planets dancing in space's ball,
Twirl and spin, they've got it all.
Mars plays drums, Jupiter sings,
Saturn brings the bling with rings!

Moons are twirling, as if on cue,
Venus saunters, saying 'How do you do?'
Neptune glows in shades of blue,
While Mercury zips—it's hard to catch, too!

Earth is grooving in slow-time beats,
While everyone's just watching their tweets.
Black holes spin like a spinning top,
If you fall in, you won't stop!

Comets slide in glitzy shoes,
Dancing through space—what a ruse!
The universe shimmies, rocks, and sways,
In timeless rhythm, it plays and plays!

Echoes Through Time

Galaxies whisper through the night,
Echoes of stars, what a delight!
Time travelers giggle, bumping heads,
"Did we just pass those ancient beds?"

Aliens laugh at our funny quirks,
"Why do they dance in strange little jerks?"
Their own moves are far more wild,
Gravity flips, and we just smiled.

Visitors wonder what's the fuss,
"Is that a comet or just a bus?"
Through wormholes, they skip and hop,
Landing softly—'Oops, forgot to stop!'

Stars take selfies, posting online,
With a hashtag: #ThisMomentIsDivine.
While echoes through time belly laugh,
At all of us trying to plot out a path!

Eclipses of Memory

I forgot my keys again, they're gone,
Did they fly away, or just move on?
They might be exploring the moon's bright side,
Or dancing where wayward shadows hide.

Yesterday's snacks, lost to the void,
Left me wondering what I destroyed.
Was it cheddar cheese or my last donut?
Cosmic mysteries in the kitchen, what a rut!

A comet raced past my chaotic chase,
Was that a speeding memory or just my face?
In the black hole of snacks, they disappear,
Eclipses of thought, yet I hold them dear.

So grab your laughs, let the echoes arise,
As I pilot through this whimsical guise.
In the cosmos of clutter, let's take a spin,
Because who would have thought I'd lose a pin?

The Song of Falling Stars

Falling stars sing lullabies at night,
But mine just whispered, "What's your plight?"
I wish for pizza or a dance with fate,
But all I get is a cosmic plate!

They twinkle and giggle, a celestial crowd,
While I fumble with wish lists, feeling loud.
"More cheese, less stress!" a star might scream,
Falling dreams that burst, not quite the cream.

As meteor showers rain down the street,
Did I just trip on my own two feet?
A waltz with gravity, oh what a sight,
Chasing wishes that vanish from light.

So let's gather stardust, and make it a show,
With cosmic giggles in high-altitude flow.
When the universe chuckles and I'm feeling clever,
Each fallen wish sings, "We're lost forever!"

Writing on the Cosmic Canvas

I picked up a crayon, it slipped from my hand,
Who knew the universe had such a plan?
Coloring black holes with very bright hues,
I created a sunset that straight-up confused.

My cosmic art looks like spilled spaghetti,
Aliens pitched in, and they're pretty petty.
"More purple! Less green!" they emphatically cheer,
While my doodles whisper, "Make us appear!"

Sketching a sun with a funky mustache,
I giggle and grin at this colorful splash.
The Milky Way's mad, taking notes on the side,
While I paint heartfelt squiggles with pride.

So let's scribble our dreams in celestial ink,
Across distant worlds where the galaxies wink.
A laugh with the stars, an artistic spree,
In this canvas of chaos, I'm finally free!

Galaxies Unraveled

In the vast expanse, I lost my sock,
It's probably hidden near an alien rock.
Galaxies spin, but where's my other shoe?
It must've traveled far, what a cosmic view!

The stars are giggling at my little plight,
Is that a nebula or just my fright?
These cosmic threads entwine and tease,
Left with one sock, oh hang on, please!

A supernova burst while I played with fate,
Did my laundry just take a stellar date?
Socks that escape to new stellar lands,
While I chase the universe with empty hands.

So here's to the cosmos, in laughter we share,
For every lost sock, a universe rare.
Galaxies chuckle, weaving stories anew,
As I wonder just how I lost that shoe!

Whispers of a Celestial Heart

In a galaxy not too far,
A comet lost its way,
It asked a star for directions,
But all they did was play.

The planets spun in dizzy dance,
With moons that went out late,
They claimed they were just stargazing,
But oh, they love to skate!

Neptune giggled, slipped, and fell,
On rings of icy blue,
While Saturn tossed the cosmic ball,
Pleading, 'Catch it if you do!'

So here's to space, with mirth and cheer,
Where gravity can't hold a grin,
Each star shares gossip, bright and clear,
In this dance where laughter's king.

Radiant Realms

In realms where sunbeams tickle dust,
And laughter trails behind,
Jupiter juggles bits of rust,
As his moons hide, misaligned.

Venus, sly, with a wink and grin,
Spills tea on the moonlit floor,
While Mars argues with the wind,
'You can't just come and soar!'

The Milky Way is a chocolate stream,
With stars that warp and bend,
Each twist a sweetly funny dream,
Where notes of joy ascend.

So let's toast to the cosmic jest,
With comets in their flight,
For in these realms, we're always blessed,
With joy that shines so bright.

The Invisible Threads of Space

Between the stars, a thread is drawn,
Connecting laughs and quirks,
Saturn's rings are worn like hats,
While Venus twirls and smirks.

A constellation's secret sign,
Is merely playful jest,
Each star a player on a line,
Each wink, a little quest.

The black holes yawn, so bored they say,
'Gravity's just a game!'
While comets paint the night away,
With trails of sparkly fame.

So here we weave our cosmic thread,
With giggles in the night,
For in this dance, where joy is bred,
We spin with pure delight.

Echoes from the Edge of Time

At the edge where time goes lazy,
And seconds try to nap,
A paradox played hide and seek,
In a cosmic catnap trap.

Eons whisper, 'Don't be late!'
As history takes a stroll,
A fractal giggles, 'What a date!'
In this cosmic, playful role.

With spacetime knitting yarns of light,
And black holes serving tea,
Each tick and tock a joke in flight,
'Come play, just wait and see!'

So let's dance through the timeless space,
Where giggles fly like kites,
For echoes from that timeless place,
Create our joyful nights.

Moonlit Musings

A cheeky moon grins wide,
While crickets play their tune,
Stars are hiccuping bright,
As night dances to June.

The owls are throwing shade,
With jokes that land like stones,
While raccoons build a parade,
In search of night-time scones.

Mice put on a ballet,
With cheese as the reward,
The moon laughs at their play,
As shadows are adored.

In this night's wild embrace,
Joy twirls in the cool air,
Laughter fills every space,
And dreams float everywhere.

Voices of the Abyss

Down in the ocean deep,
Where fish wear tiny hats,
An octopus takes a leap,
And bubbles fall like spats.

The crabs throw a wild ball,
With seaweed as their prize,
While turtles try to crawl,
In synchronized dumb-fies.

Whales sing a funny tune,
That rattles coral's bones,
While jellyfish float soon,
And giggle near the stones.

Gigglefits rise and swell,
In this deep-sea delight,
Where antics cast a spell,
Beneath the waves at night.

The Symphony of Spheres

Planets in a silly race,
Around the sun they spin,
Mars is losing face,
Jupiter starts to grin.

Venus throws a grand ball,
With asteroids as guests,
Saturn's rings are tall,
While Uranus wears vests.

Neptune, the cool cat,
Sips stars through a long straw,
While comets do a spat,
And cheer with lots of 'raw!'

The solar system's fun,
With laughs echoing wide,
In galactic old run,
Dad jokes on their side.

Dreamscapes of Distant Worlds

In dreams of far-off lands,
Small aliens pull pranks,
With candy in their hands,
And silly tanky tanks.

They skateboard on their moons,
With giggles filling air,
While space cats sing old tunes,
And twirl without a care.

The clouds throw fluffy pies,
That leave a tasty mess,
While planets wink their eyes,
At this galactic fest.

In these dreams quite absurd,
Where joy takes flight and whirls,
A canvas yet unheard,
In mind's fun, distant swirls.

Stardust Chronicles

Once a comet lost its tail,
It wandered off and told a tale.
In quasar cafes, they'd laugh and play,
While asteroids danced the night away.

Mars tried to flirt with a passing star,
But it blushed and said, 'You're too far!'
Venus rolled her eyes with flair,
'Quit your whining, it's only air!'

Black holes held a cosmic ball,
Where no one laughed, but they had a ball.
Jupiter sighed, 'I'm just too big!'
While Saturn spun in a dazzling jig.

So gather 'round, celestial friends,
The universe giggles and never ends.
In this vast expanse of cosmic jest,
Even the aliens need a rest!

Celestial Ballet

The moon slipped on her sparkly dress,
While Mars tried hard to impress.
Stars twirled in their cosmic shoes,
Whispering secrets like they were news.

Cassiopeia tripped on her crown,
And Pluto just chuckled, rolling down.
Galaxies twisted in pirouette,
As comets giggled, 'Ain't this a bet?'

Neptune hummed a watery tune,
While Uranus danced like a cartoon.
The asteroids formed a clumsy line,
Bumping and bouncing, looking just fine.

So let's all sway 'neath this starry dome,
In this funny ballet, we find a home.
With each twirl, a laugh made clear,
In the dance of the spheres, let's all cheer!

Among the Constellations

In the sky, Orion lost his belt,
And giggled hard, oh what a felt!
Ursa Major threw a bear-y great bash,
While the Little Dipper spilled space-ish trash.

Andromeda said, 'I'm quite the view!'
But the stars replied, 'We see right through!'
They laughed and pointed with starry fingers,
As a supernova burst, and laughter lingers.

Some stars plotted their cosmic pranks,
While others offered their shining thanks.
For in the dark, a light shines bright,
When constellations meet on a starry night.

So let's not take our sky so serious,
For in this vast realm, it's mysterious.
With jokes and jests among the beams,
We find our joy midst the cosmic dreams!

Silence Between Stars

Between each star, a whisper hums,
An echo of laughter from distant drums.
The silence shatters with meteors' calls,
As comets buzz past like rambunctious balls.

'Why so quiet?' the Earthlings muse,
While gravity pulls on cosmic shoes.
Venus sighed, 'We've got no plans,'
Yet truly, the stars are biggest fans.

Galaxy clusters play hide and seek,
While Saturn's rings have a sly little peek.
The void giggles with barely a sound,
As the universe spins round and round.

So lift your head to the night so deep,
With the humorous light that keeps us from sleep.
In the silence, find joy in the sight,
Of the vast cosmos, both funny and bright!

Cosmic Dialogues

In the cosmos, stars start to chat,
A comet's saying, "Look at that!"
Black holes whisper, "We're so deep,"
While asteroids prank, causing a beep.

Galaxies gossip, swirling in pairs,
Neptune wears a hat; oh, who cares?
The moon grins wide at Earth below,
"Dance with me, let's put on a show!"

Mars teases Venus, "You're too bright!"
She retorts, "At least I'm not a fright!"
Saturn laughs, his rings all twirl,
Then gives Uranus quite a swirl.

In this vast expanse, laughter does ring,
As planets trade jokes, like old friends in spring.
So next time you gaze at the celestial dance,
Remember the humor in their cosmic romance.

Universe in Verses

In a galaxy far, the stars threw a party,
But dancing comets were feeling quite tardy.
The sun got up, took center stage,
And laughed at the planets, "Get in your cage!"

Jupiter, hefty, tried to take flight,
While Mercury zoomed with hilarious might.
"Watch me orbit!" said Earth with a spin,
But tripped on its axis, what a clumsy grin!

Neptune said, "Guys, let's have a game!"
"Who can stay cool?" they all played the same.
But Mars called foul, "That's just unfair!"
While everyone floated in laughter and air.

Together they'd spin in their funny ballet,
A universe penned in a comical way.
So next time you wonder what they might say,
Just imagine their giggles stretching night and day.

Gravity's Embrace

Gravity chuckled, pulling things near,
"You can run, but I'm always right here!"
Planets cling tightly, just hanging around,
While moons spin in circles, feeling so sound.

Astronauts float, but oh what a sight,
Chasing their tools, they wiggle with fright.
"Is that a wrench?" one shouts with delight,
As it drifts past the window, a dance in the night.

Saturn just grinned, his rings all aglow,
"Look at these moves, oh don't be so slow!"
But Earth rolled its eyes, "You think you can tease?
I have seasons that change; you'd fall to your knees!"

In this playful pull, the planets find glee,
While gravity serves up its funny decree.
So next time you trip or feel a light trace,
Remember it's all in gravity's embrace.

Echoes from a Distant Star

A twinkling star sent a giggle so grand,
To planets below, drifting through sand.
"Hey there, Earth, feeling a bit blue?"
"Just look to the sky, there's plenty to do!"

Venus replied, a wink in her light,
"We dance and we shine, it's a fabulous sight!"
The star chuckled back, "Oh, don't you know?
I collect all your laughter, let it glow!"

In this vast ocean of cosmic delight,
Echoes travel far, keeping spirits bright.
A wave to the moon, then a wink to Mars,
In the dance of the night, they swing with the stars.

So when you gaze up at the shimmering night,
Remember the echoes that take joyful flight.
For laughter among stars is a wonderful truth,
And it travels through space, like eternal youth.

The Space Between Breath

In lungs of gas and cosmic air,
I float around without a care.
Breath in, breath out, a silly game,
Who knew the sky had such a name?

I counted stars, then lost the count,
They giggle back; they're in a roundabout.
My wheezy laugh, a comet's trail,
Echoes in realms, beyond the pale.

Each gasp is like a bouncing ball,
Who knew the void could hear my call?
With every inhale, quirks arise,
This universe? A grand surprise!

So here I'll float, on laughter's breeze,
Between the stars and cosmic sneeze.
Inhale the fun, exhale the grind,
In this space, joy's never confined.

Dance of the Orbiting Minds

Round and round, we spin and swirl,
Like kids who give their tops a twirl.
In the galaxy's goofy groove,
Our thoughts create a cosmic move.

Planets tangle in a silly race,
Chasing tails in a cluttered space.
With each idea, they twist and twine,
In this carnival, we're all divine.

A comet does the cha-cha-cha,
While aliens sip green beverages—a big hurrah!
Quantum leaps with a bounce and wiggle,
In the galaxy, it's all a giggle.

So join the dance, come take a chance,
In this vast void, we prance and dance.
With every thought, let laughter reign,
In orbit's grip, we lose the mundane.

Craters of Thought

In my mind are craters, deep and vast,
Filled with ideas that come in a blast.
I trip on logic, then take a fall,
Laughing at echoes that bounce off the wall.

Each crater whispers secrets old,
Of dreams that glitter and stories bold.
From tiny sparks, a fireworks show,
In this cosmic brain, ideas grow.

Oh, the impact left by a stone!
Where did it land? I once had known.
A wild guess, but who really cares?
They laugh like children in cosmic fairs.

So let's explore this lunar maze,
Where thoughts erupt in a wacky daze.
Craters of wonder, craters of glee,
In the universe, it's just you and me!

A Journey through the Starlit Abyss

Through the abyss, I take a ride,
On a rocket of dreams, with laughter inside.
Stars are winking, all aglow,
Playing peekaboo while I'm below.

Gravity plays a funny trick,
Pulling at me with a cosmic flick.
"Hey, I'm up here, come join the fun!"
I bounce around like a wayward gun.

The dark is filled with giggles bright,
As lunar mice come out at night.
They dance on asteroids, play hide and seek,
Their little tummies, oh so sleek!

So let's journey through this twinkling scene,
Where absurd becomes our jumping bean.
In this starlit void where dreams can sigh,
We'll chase the shadows and laugh till we fly!

Nightfall's Wisdom

The moon in the sky took a dive,
Grinning as stars began to arrive.
They twinkled and winked, oh what a sight,
Saying, "We work best when it's night!"

Raccoons got busy, donned masks and capes,
Planning their heists with goofy shapes.
While owls swapped gossip, wise as can be,
"Who's hooting at whom? Let's have some tea!"

The comet whizzed by with a tail full of cheer,
It said, "Hold my beer, I'm not done here!"
With a sonic boom, it wrote in the sky,
A cartoon of aliens waving goodbye.

In dreams, we all dance, in pajamas galore,
Floating like leaves through the cosmic floor.
As nightfall descends, we all laugh and play,
Wiser by midnight, at least for the day!

Solar Serenades

The sun threw a party, all bright and bold,
With rays of gold and warmth to behold.
Clouds danced above, looking quite high,
Waving their hands like, "Oh my, oh my!"

The planets all showed up, each in their style,
Venus wore glitter and Jupiter smiled.
Saturn spun tales of its ring parade,
While Mars argued loudly, "I'm not afraid!"

A solar flare belted out a tune,
As comets joined in, twirling the moon.
The light was contagious, laughter spread wide,
Even the asteroids joined in with pride!

As dusk crept in, they said, "What a blast!
We'll do this again, let's make it a fest!"
With a wink and a grin, the sun took its bow,
A solar serenade, we'll remember somehow!

The Dance of Planets

In a cosmic ballroom, the planets align,
Each one in step, with a frothy wine.
Earth laughed aloud, "Watch me do the twist!"
While Pluto complained, "I'm always dismissed!"

Mercury zipped by, all speedy and spry,
"Hold on to your hats, just watch me fly!"
And Venus, the diva, swung her hips bold,
Said, "Stop all that fuss, I'm purest gold!"

Neptune was dreaming, lost in a trance,
With waves in his head, he forgot the dance.
Uranus, quite quirky, brought sparkly feet,
With laughter and bubbles, he couldn't be beat.

As the music crescendoed, a supernova blast,
Galaxies spun as this party grew vast.
The planets all cheered, each twirling with glee,
In the dance of the universe, wild and free!

Moonlit Epiphanies

Under the moon, thoughts spark and gleam,
Ideas burst forth like a wild daydream.
"Why do we park our spacecraft on grass?
Next time, let's park on the rings of Saturn, alas!"

Stars chimed in with giggles and light,
"Let's plan a road trip to visit the night!"
Venus suggested a game of charades,
While Mars shook its head, "I'd rather throw grenades!"

In this cosmic café where wisdom is free,
Galaxies pondered, "What's full and what's three?"
And why does that black hole look so confused?
"Is it hungry for something? Did it get bruised?"

When laughter winds down and the night wears thin,
We find tiny joys stored deep within.
Moonlit epiphanies wrap us so tight,
Bringing whispers of joy in the silence of night!

Starlit Chronicles

In a galaxy not too far,
A cat tried to reach a star.
It leaped and missed, fell from the sky,
Then landed softly with a sigh.

A dog once wore a spacey hat,
Claiming he'd chat with a friendly bat.
But the bat flew off to find some bees,
Leaving the dog confused with ease.

Aliens came to fix their ship,
But wasted time on a cosmic trip.
They stopped for ice cream on a comet,
And danced, while leaving out their sonnet.

Stars giggle, planets play,
In this vast, strange cabaret.
Oh, how the universe loves a jest,
Beyond the moon, it never rests.

The Gravity of Thoughts

My mind feels heavy, like a black hole,
Sucking in all that's in my scroll.
Ideas collide with a cosmic crash,
Like popcorn popping in a hyper fast bash.

Quasars whisper secrets of the skies,
While I just wonder about missed pies.
Gravity pulls me to my chair,
As I daydream of a more daring affair.

Asteroids crash with a clattering sound,
While I just sit and stroll around.
Meteors go zooming without a care,
As I struggle to find my underwear.

Thoughts float like balloons in the air,
But I can't chase 'em, it's just not fair.
So here I sit, all tied in knots,
Wondering why I forgot my thoughts.

Orbiting Dreams

Dreams orbit me like moons in flight,
Some are rascals, some feel right.
One wants candy, another a race,
While another just wants to chill in space.

I tossed a wish to Jupiter's ring,
But it bounced back, gave me a sting.
The planets laughed, spun in jest,
While I just hoped for a cosmic fest.

Saturn's up there, giving me shade,
As I try to catch a running spade.
Venus blows kisses, then swiftly hides,
Leaving me stranded by the asteroid slides.

With dreams so wild, they twist and twirl,
I just hope they won't give me a whirl.
So I sit back, enjoy the view,
And chuckle at the chaos that flew.

Tides of Celestial Ink

With pens that write of stars and spice,
I dip them in the salt of nice.
A comet's tail becomes my quill,
As I scribble dreams with cosmic thrill.

Galaxies spin like a merry-go-round,
As I laugh at words that make no sound.
The moon chuckles with a knowing glow,
As I scratch my head, trying to flow.

Eclipses hide in silly disguise,
While I write nonsense that surely flies.
Supernovae burst with laughter loud,
As I misplace my thoughts in a cloud.

Tides of ink rise, splatter and fall,
Creating a tune in the cosmic hall.
So come and join this droll parade,
Where the universe giggles and dreams are made.

Nebula Narratives

In a cloud of dust, a tale took flight,
Starfish giggled under the moonlight.
Cosmic babies danced in a zero-gravity way,
While asteroids played hide-and-seek all day.

A comet sneezed, a bright tail did soar,
With each little giggle, we wanted more.
Mars wore sunglasses, fancied a show,
Jupiter juggled moons; what a cosmic flow!

Uranus chuckled, what a cheeky tease,
Twirled as it spun on that galactic breeze.
Neptune told jokes, not a single sigh,
While everyone laughed till they cracked a pie!

In this universe, laughter is grand,
With stars shining bright, hand in hand.
So float in the cosmos, let joy take a bow,
In these nebula narratives, let fun be our vow!

Stellar Reflections

In the mirror of space, stars preen and pose,
Twirling their tails, striking a pose.
Saturn's rings blinged with a wink and a nod,
As the Milky Way giggled; isn't it odd?

Light-years away, they'd sip cosmic tea,
Chit-chatting atoms, so fancy and free.
With black holes that burp, oh what a surprise,
Absorbing all snacks from the grand cosmic pies.

The sun tried to dance, but got too much heat,
While planets rolled by in their shiny elite.
'Let's keep it light!' shouted a fun-loving quasar,
As they zoomed through the universe, happy and bizarre.

In stellar reflections, craziness reigns,
With stars in tuxedos, and laughter with gains.
So who needs gravity when you can have fun,
In the dance of the cosmos, we're all number one!

Astral Stories Underneath

Beneath the stars where the comets zip,
Frogs in tuxedos planned a grand trip.
They hopped on asteroids with all their might,
Sipping stardust smoothies, what a delight!

Martians played poker at the moonlit's edge,
While Venusians joked, 'We made a hedge!'
Earth's critters swung high on a cosmic swing,
Laughing and twirling, what joy it did bring.

Saturn, the prankster, glued on some glue,
Caught over-eager stars, oh what a view!
While black holes spun tales of wild ride-ins,
Even the meteors joined in the din.

In these astral stories, laughter ignites,
With winks from the Milky Way, adding delights.
So gather your giggles, let the fun begin,
In the cosmic playground, we'll all fit in!

The Language of Light

In photons and giggles, we find our stride,
With sunbeams chuckling, what a wild ride!
Each ray a messenger, with jokes to impart,
Luminous puns dancing, brightening the heart.

Light beams travel fast, but humor travels more,
Flirting with shadows on a cosmic dance floor.
Eclipses took selfies, turned dark then bright,
Twinkling in laughter through the depths of night.

Supernova parties, a riotous affair,
Exploding with joy, leaving stardust in the air.
While pulsars tick-tocked in rhythm sublime,
Each flash a giggle, each pulse a rhyme.

In the language of light, where fun finds a home,
Galaxies whisper, together we roam.
So let's shine and sparkle as we orbit this place,
In this whimsical universe, let laughter embrace!

Fragments of Starlight

In the night, stars play peek-a-boo,
Twinkling like kids in a cosmic zoo.
They whisper secrets, giggle with glee,
Making wishes as wild as can be.

Planets spin tales in their orbiting dance,
Like awkward friends at a cosmic romance.
Mars brings cookies, while Venus sings loud,
Saturn's rings dazzle, standing proud.

Neptune's the sea with its deep, swirling jokes,
While Jupiter's storms just tickle with pokes.
They chuckle and twirl in the vast, silly space,
Where each little quasar has its own happy face.

And as comets streak past with a glittering trail,
They all yell, "Catch us if you can!" in the gale.
So here's to the fragments that light up the night,
Each twinkle a laugh, a pure, sparkling sight.

Cosmic Conversations

In the sky, stars chat over cosmic tea,
They gossip and giggle; oh, what rivalry!
Orion teases, "I'm the best with my bow!"
While Scorpio snaps back, "Just watch me glow!"

The Moon joins in, with a grin so wide,
"Hey, don't forget who steers the tide!"
Mars brags about his rusty red flair,
"Who needs rings? I'm beyond compare!"

A black hole jokes, "I'm a real vacuum!"
"Just suck in the light; I'm the star of the room!"
While asteroids roll in, bumping and crashing,
Telling tales of adventures, all crashing and flashing.

And as the milky waves flow soft through the night,
Galaxies swirl in a dance of delight.
So here's to the banter that echoes above,
A theater of laughter, a story of love.

Dance of the Celestials

Celestial friends in a waltz up high,
Jupiter twirls, making comets sigh.
While Saturn pirouettes with rings so fine,
"Just look at my bling, isn't it divine?"

The Sun is a DJ with solar beats,
Spinning rays that get everyone on their feet.
Venus, the dancer, sways to the sound,
Her luminescence lighting up the ground.

Uranus, the joker, rolls on its side,
"Why stand up straight? I prefer the slide!"
While Pluto the underdog proudly states,
"I may be small, but I still bring the greats!"

In the cosmic disco, they all take a chance,
With stars as the audience, in a marvelous dance.
For in this wild party, there's no need for rest,
Just celestial laughter and a groove to invest.

Veins of the Earth

Deep in the ground, where the gnomes like to dwell,
They squabble over treasure, a shiny hard shell.
Roots laugh and wiggle, tickled by rain,
While worms in the soil sing a squishy refrain.

Mountains stand sturdy like grumpy old folks,
With boulders that mumble their ancient dad jokes.
Rivers giggle past, trickling with cheer,
"Catch me if you can! I'm the fastest right here!"

Grass blades compete in a green-growing race,
Tickling the toes of each human they face.
Trees share their gossip, rustling their leaves,
"Did you hear about the oak? He's as tall as he believes!"

So, here's to the veins that pulse life to the crust,
Each rocky and rooty, in nature we trust.
For beneath and above, it's all a grand play,
A funny old world, in its own quirky way.

Tides of Time and Space

There once was a time with no clocks at all,
Existed in chaos, what a comedy thrall.
The sun wore a hat, the moon danced in glee,
Stars giggled like children, oh-so-free!

Gravity's pranks kept us jumping around,
Upside down cities with laughter abound.
A fish flew by waving its fin like a wand,
In this space-time mix-up, we're all so fond!

Sometimes we trip on the past, what a tease,
While future predictions are just a few keys.
The cosmos, a circus, each planet a clown,
In the grand show of life, we all wear the crown!

So grab your time-travelers, pack up your snacks,
Get ready to laugh as the universe cracks.
With each little giggle, the worlds start to spin,
Tides of time, oh what a whimsical grin!

Aeons in Verse

Once there was a comet, with a tail made of cake,
As it flew through the heavens, it started to bake.
Planets all drooled; they could hardly behave,
"Bring us a slice!" they cried, oh so brave!

Stars wrote their stories in frosting and sprinkles,
And moons spun around, doing their twinkly twinkles.
Jupiter danced with a skip and a jump,
While Saturn served drinks with a fizzy ol' thump!

Aeons of laughter stretch throughout the space,
We're all just the cast in this cosmic embrace.
With quips from quasars and jokes from black holes,
Life on these orbs is for giggling souls!

So next time you gaze at the vast, starry night,
Remember the humor that twinkles so bright.
Across endless verses, we frolic and play,
In the game of existence, it's all just a sway!

Shadows of the Infinite

In the depths of the cosmos, shadows start to slip,
A dance of mischief from a celestial trip.
Asteroids tap-danced, meteorites winked,
While galaxies giggled, as they softly linked.

A black hole had a party, invited the light,
"Come join the fun, it's a stellar delight!"
But light got too dizzy, and vanished like sneeze,
Now it just hides in the fabric of tease.

Eons grew younger, while time became bold,
And comets told tales that never got old.
In this shadowy dance, the universe plays,
With each little wink, the night turns to days!

Remember to laugh at the cosmic parade,
For shadows are just where the light has delayed.
In the infinite laughter, we find our embrace,
Echoes of humor fill infinite space!

Illuminated Journeys

Rocket ships chuckling, flying through clouds,
Tickling the stars, oh, laughter so loud!
Planets in pajamas join in the spree,
Navigating cosmos, just feeling so free.

Nebulae wear shades, keeping cool in the void,
With comical echoes of laughter enjoyed.
Riding light beams, the universe sings,
As quarks giggle sweetly, oh the joy that it brings!

Cosmic whirlwinds of jest swirl all around,
In this dance of the skies, it's humor we've found.
Galaxies humorously spin out of place,
In a funny ballet, with infinite grace!

So pack up your joy and set course without fear,
On this journey of stars, where all laughter is clear.
The humor of space is a treasure galore,
Illuminated journeys, forever explore!

www.ingramcontent.com/pod-product-compliance
Lightning Source LLC
Chambersburg PA
CBHW071843160426
43209CB00003B/398